THE 30-DAY SPEAK LIFE CHALLENGE

#30DaySpeakLifeChallenge
#30DSLC

Deborah C. Quave

Copyright © 2017
by Deborah C. Quave, Use Your Words Publishing

All rights reserved. In accordance with the U.S. Copyright Act of 1976, the scanning, uploading, and electronic sharing of any part of this book without the permission of the publisher constitute unlawful piracy and theft of the author's intellectual property.
If you would like to use material from the book (other than for review purposes), prior written permission must be obtained by contacting the publisher at info@useyourwordsthemovement.com. Thank you for your support of the author's rights.

The 30-Day Speak Life Challenge
Published in the United States of America by
Use Your Words Publishing
Moss Point, MS 39563

ISBN: **978-0-9987006-1-8**

All Scriptures quotations are from the Amplified Everyday Life Bible by Joyce Meyer, copyright © 2014

Cover and Graphic Design by
Rhonda Delgado of Rhonda Delgado Designs

Interior and Layout by Shanmugapriya Balasubramanian

Printed in the United States of America

All rights reserved.

DEDICATION

To every person who has ever battled in the fight of depression, known insecurity, been plagued with inadequacy; I see you, I feel you, I am...

you.

Acknowledgments

Though I could never cover them all, I would like to thank everyone who has been called upon to edit an extremely long text or email in the middle of the night. To every friend who has FaceTimed me "in the closet" and let me cry out the pain of this process, your gift of time is invaluable. The genuine support I have received since beginning the Use Your Words journey to completing this work has been unfounded. In life they say if we meet one or two close friends then you have done well, I think I have done great...

To my Savior, Provider, and Friend, my love for you runs deep. And yet still, I cannot comprehend your love for me. May you continue the Good Work I see...

To Grandma Elverdia, thank you for letting me rock out with you in L.A. as God broke the ground for this new dimension in my life. Our time and your words will never be forgotten. I am standing on the shoulders of many and am lifted by the prayers of my ancestors. "Still I rise"...

To my family: Mom & Dad, Greg, Chastity, Patricia, Daniel, and Mykhael the journey's been wild. May your understanding of self be greater, may our love grow stronger. I love you forever...

To my nieces and nephews: Damarian, Brittany, Maci, Ayden, Jeremiah, and the many more to come, may you roam this earth loudly, may your spirits stay free, may your soar surpass the heavens. Auntie DeeDee loves you...

Mrs. Nita, you have beckoned this writer for many years. Thank you for always believing, speaking, encouraging, laughing, and doing it all over again and again. Your "whisper" has been my life's "epiphany"...

Jason & Shug, thank you for opening your hearts and home as the Wind blew me to you. If it were not for the "closet" and the movie room this book could not exist. Thank you for letting me takeover the walls with my sticky notes. Thank you for joining in my dance and feeding me tacos and fresh-sausage. Most of all, thank you for being crazy enough to let me and JuneBug take care of each other...

Baby Junior, you helped me to heal. We cried together and boy did we laugh. We grew together in infancy, you made me braver than I ever knew I could be...

To Rebecca James, in a crowd of 20,000 people God knew you'd be there to help me in my darkest hour. You taught me how to stand on the Word and speak life when I wanted to die; thank you for insisting that Jesus Lords over the enemy. The world and body of Christ need more compassionate, indignant pastoral leaders and counselors as you. You are powerful in your job and you do it well...

To my "Los Angeles" Bay Area sisters: from another mister, Marisa and Luckie: When God gave me the two of you, He gave me my birth sisters all over again. Since the inception of Use Your Words, you have both faithfully stood by my side. Your support and friendship have undergirded me as Aaron and Hur did Moses; for that I am grateful...

Marisa, there are not adequate words to describe the type of forward momentum you have brought into my life. Deep down I always felt I could accomplish great things, however, your friendship has helped me to believe that I am capable of conquering the world. From moving and flying across the US with me, you have been my soul-sister and I thank you for accepting me face value from the very start. We met broken and bruised, literally. It has been an honor to watch God put the pieces of both our lives together, the right way. Thank you for always asking, "Have you been writing?" It was when I did not want to do it that you pushed the hardest, I'm thankful...

Luckie, we met on the premise of me walking in blind-faith and our friendship continues that theme. From debuting our media careers on the Red Carpet of L.A., to blazing the streets of New York City, you continue to remind me, "You're His daughter, God's gotta take care of you". Thanks for trusting my crazy ventures and never judging the way I follow His path...

To my brothers from another mother, Shawn, Jonathan and Emmett: Thanks for showing me how "God's daughters" should be treated. It has been said, "men and women can't be just friends", I think we've shown them differently...

Shawn, your presence in my life has mattered since the beginning. From capturing my first speaking engagement in Los Angeles to launching the Use Your Words prayer call in your living room, at conception you made it clear that you had my back. Thank you for being my friend without obligation and for challenging me to follow the God-path. You're one of a kind...

Jonathan, thanks for asking the hard questions and requiring an answer. Your words of life built me up in my darkest hours. Thanks for being a constant support to Use Your Words and my visions. Thanks for being unafraid to tell me the truth at all times...

Emmett, from the bright halls of The College of Business at Southern Miss to traversing the tides of adulthood, I am grateful for your consistency in my life. Thank you for being genuine and always supporting my visions and dreams, especially as it relates to Use Your Words...

To my line sister and fellow scribe Gracie, may your "Thawts" and my "Words" continue to heal the deeply wounded. Thank you for every shared tear, laugh, and moment of encouragement. You are a rock...

To my publishing team: Rhonda & Kandi, thank you for jumping in the trenches with me and ensuring this work was birthed properly. Your excellence and commitment to every detail was amazing to witness...

Rhonda, oh Rhonda! I am convinced God gifted you with the same creative eye as He. Your design ability blows me away every time. I am so thankful for the ball of energy you bring to the Use Your Words family. Thanks for taking this on in such a short period of time. Your courage to dive into this challenge while embracing every obstacle is to be admired. I pray your greatest desires are fulfilled as you continue to design for the masses. Love you!...

Kandi, my dear friend, Kandi...the last leg of this journey could not have been completed without you. Thank you for being my editor. Thank you for believing in my passion and joining the team with supreme excellence and dedication. Thank you for your voice of wisdom and reason. It looks like I have finally learned, "how to fly"...

Contents

Acknowledgments---v
Foreword---xi
Introduction -- xiii

Day 1
At All Costs--1

Day 2
It's Empty for a Reason--5

Day 3
Steps of Peace--11

Day 4
It's in Your Hands -- 15

Day 5
Out with the Old, In with the New------------------------------- 21

Day 6
Truthful Realities-- 27

Day 7
End in Praise--- 31

Day 8
Is God Enough?--- 35

Day 9
Love Takes Risk --- 41

Day 10
You are Special --- 45

Day 11
Press Play --49

Day 12
The Grind of Faith--- 53

Day 13
Strength in Weakness-- 57

Day 14
The God of Restoration, Renewal, and Peace ------------------- 61

Day 15
Glimpses of Yesterday --- 67

Day 16
Purge-- 71
Day 17
Dark Places-- 75
Day 18
New Things -- 79
Day 19
Focus on the Happy-- 85
Day 20
Free the Power-- 93
Day 21
Moments that Matter -- 97
Day 22
Believe in the Work You Do ---103
Day 23
Protect the Gifts --109
Day 24
The Requirement of Worship -- 115
Day 25
Get Up and Go --- 121
Day 26
Come and Take ---125
Day 27
God Will Help You ---129
Day 28
Major in the Minor---129
Day 29
Faith-Forward Progression--- 135
Day 30
Rise -- 141

Conclusion ---144
About the Author --147
Contact --149

Foreword

We are living in an era where it seems as if the world has gone mad. There is an abuse and overuse of creative tools meant to enhance forms of communication. Tools such as social media can have an adverse effect on how people communicate. It is a large contributing factor to the decline of human-to-human communication. Many people simply talk about, talk around, and talk at each other instead of virtuously communicating their successes, flaws, and/or grievances. This predicament is not confined to any single race, religion, gender, or socioeconomic status. It has permeated cracks and crevices that previously have been impenetrable. If ever there was a time to "Use Your Words", it is now!

I have known Deborah Quave, affectionately called Deedee, since she was a teenager in high school. My husband moved our family to her birthplace of record "good ole' Mississippi." I met her mother and we became friends. I immediately knew that God had assigned me and my husband to her family for a season. I had been praying for and rooting for Deborah long before she ever knew or understood the value of our relationship. As years passed, I have had the pleasure to unconditionally love her, laboriously mentor her, and humbly grow to call her friend. It has been an honor to watch her blossom into this effervescent, beautiful flower; a beauty that tirelessly colors and freshens the Kingdom of God. She has been on a quest to facilitate better communication with her God, family, friends, and ultimately the world.

Deborah understands how imperative it is to speak life into every situation. Barraged by many obstacles and setbacks, I have watched this young woman fight constantly to ensure she fulfills her dreams and divine destiny. Speaking life is not just a part of her debut book; it has become a part of her daily lifeline. She is challenging us to usher efficient communication to the forefront once again.

Clear communication has been and always will be the concrete adhesive that binds every worthwhile relationship. *The 30-Day Speak Life Challenge* will arouse us to positive change. It is essential for us to build confidence in ourselves, establish relational foundation with our Creator, and reconstruct community with one another. *The 30-Day Speak Life Challenge* delivers just that! This is a book to share with your family, your friends, and even your enemies. I believe Deborah's desire is for this challenge to turn into a lifetime of consistent and effective communication that is propelling as well as wholistic. I hope you are ready for this transformation; I most certainly am!

Paulette Thompson, Life Coach
United States Air Force Veteran
Illinois
2017

Introduction

Hello There!

Only God could have you writing about speaking *life* during the most mentally difficult time of your life. This book was birthed as a tool to save my own life. It came during a time when I was in counseling, dealing with mental health issues, and struggling to retain emotional stability. I wrote this work for myself and those like me, facing depression, anxiety, and some of life's most challenging obstacles. I felt compelled to release this "first of many" projects after coming to terms with the fact that I have felt insignificant, insecure, and inadequate for the majority of my life. I saw this step as a way to defeat the negativity that has tormented me for decades. My resolve was that, publicly exposing my scars could have the potential to help someone else. I pray it does.

As you read through the text, it is my hope that you dare to be open and honest. I hope this book causes you to seek and establish meaningful, healthy connections in your life. It is my prayer that upon the completion of your journey with me, you would have established not only a new way of thinking and speaking, but most importantly, a new way of living. One that promotes positivity, self-acceptance, and builds its foundation on the Word of God, not the lies and suggestions of Satan. Satan wants us to believe that our lives can never change for the better. However I now *know* that is not true. God, who spoke this world into existence, has instilled into us a power to speak that will bring our world under His divine order and into this earthly realm.

The thing I have learned about the Word of God is that it is not as useful if it is not spoken. Do not get me wrong, reading it helps, but if it is not spoken it is not producing the life we desire. The Bible says, "Faith comes by hearing and hearing by the Word of God". Well, you cannot hear what you do not say. When we speak, we subconsciously hear what we are saying. So when we say, "I can't", unknowingly we have placed limitations on our abilities to complete a task. When we say, "It's killing me", we are literally yielding portions of our being to a death that can only be caused by the surrendering of our words to a negative, non-life giving rhetoric.

In closing, thank you for allowing me into the secrecy of your life; into the most precious quadrants of your living space, your mind. It is my prayer that the God of this universe would unite with us and reveal great truths to you and me as we prepare to change our lives for the better. I am grateful that you are on this journey with me. It is sure to be an experience that will revolutionize the way we speak to ourselves, while at the same time helping us to cultivate an "I can...I will...end of story" attitude!

ABOUT THE CHALLENGE

I created *The 30-Day Speak Life Challenge* in the summer of 2014. Originally coined The 30-Day Reflection Experiment, it has since evolved into a fundamental tool for exposing how we presently relate to the world from our unique human experiences. I found from traveling across the country, between 2013 to 2016, that self-inflicted wounds are the greatest barriers to positive self-progression. I noticed that many people, like myself, often lift others up while terrorizing and tearing ourselves down. As a result, I was motivated to write this book to help encourage us all, through the art of communication, to be more kind to ourselves on this journey of life.

WHAT YOU WILL NEED

The 30-Day Speak Life Challenge book
A mirror
A journal and a pen

HOW IT WORKS

There are thirty chapters in this book, hence *The 30-Day Speak Life Challenge*. Each chapter consists of a body of the text, a 'Deb Download' and a 'Mirror Challenge'. Every day we will complete the daily reading, the Deb Download (which is used to summarize the lesson or key takeaway from the content of each day), then the Mirror Challenge. The Mirror Challenge serves as a time of reflection. It is a time, at least 60 seconds, where we come face-to-face with who we are and learn more about ourselves. This is also the time where we will be speaking life to ourselves everyday... for thirty days. Are you ready?

Let's go!

Yours in His Service,

AT ALL COSTS

"I do not consider, brethren, that I have captured and made it my own [yet]; but one thing I do [it is my one aspiration]: forgetting what lies behind and straining forward to what lies ahead."

–Philippians 3:13

Because we live in a world with so many options, I believe a great part of our generation lacks the character it takes to complete what we start. Sticking to one thing; a relationship, job, vehicle, apartment, city, or state is no longer the norm. The problem with this is, we translate these fickle habits directly into the principles in our relationship with God. Let us take the spiritual principle of fasting for example. We fast as a way to abstain from an indulgence in order to grow closer to God and get clarity. On a fast, it is easy to quit, change the rules midway, or cheat. Believe me, I know this because I have done them all. However, one of the main benefits of fasting is the discipline acquired from staying committed to the experience of the process.

In many ways, this challenge is like a fast. We are intentionally avoiding negative thinking and speaking by replacing them with positive affirmations of truth through God's Word. For some, this may be simple, but for many, this is a tough task. As we journey through this process, it is important to establish the parameters of what we are trying to accomplish.

If you are like me and have dealt with issues in finishing what you start, look to our role model Paul. He put all of his efforts into becoming better by "straining forward". This implies that there was a struggle. However, Paul was more eager to complete his assignment than allowing it to remain incomplete. When you find yourself getting weak or inconsistent throughout this challenge refer back to your written reasons for engaging in this task. Our journey to greatness started with our ability to keep promises to ourselves and to the God of this universe.

DEB'S DOWNLOAD

Finish it.

MIRROR CHALLENGE

Ask yourself the following questions, then write your answers in your journal.

1. *Why am I doing this challenge?*
2. *What do I want to accomplish?*
3. *What am I asking of God during this time?*
4. *How do I want to be better by the end of this process?*

Finish this challenge with a prayer aloud.

IT'S EMPTY FOR A REASON

"He is not here; He has risen, as He said [He would do]. Come, see the place where He lay."

–Matthew 28:6

My journey with God began when I was eight years old. I recall being on the swing set during recess at College Park Elementary, in my hometown, Gautier, Mississippi, when I first heard the voice of God. From then on, and all throughout my scholastic years, my relationship with God was truly "an ever-present help". So it was an absolute surprise when, after college, I found myself standing at the gate of unbelief.

At this time in my early twenties, living in Los Angeles, and being exposed to new ways of thinking, I found myself unsure if what I had been holding as Truth was still accurate. During this time, every area of my life was up for questioning. After many conversations, lectures, and in depth theological discussions, I recognized that somehow I had become an emotional creature of habit instead of a disciplined follower of Truth. The toughest moment for me occurred when I had to admit that I did not really believe that Jesus rose from the dead. The pain that followed this discovery was intolerable. What did this mean? Was I not a Christian? Did I make Jesus mad by my admission of uncertain belief? Where did He and I stand from this point on?

The days and weeks following this revelation came with unprecedented amounts of studying historical documents, reading the Bible, self-inquiry, prayers, online research, and conversations with professors and mentors who were not afraid to help aide me in my arrival to Truth. I decided that in order to gain a better understanding of my position in Faith, I needed to go where Jesus lived. So in 2011, I took my first trip abroad to Israel. I gained a plethora of knowledge about the man, Jesus.

The first thing I learned is his real name is Yeshua. A second revelation was the fact that, in Israel, people talked about Yeshua as a person. His life became real to me. To see where He grew up, His family design and structure, and tracing historically significant moments before the Cross erased the mythology surrounded in the figure of the Jesus we have created in the western world.

The most impactful moment occurred for me toward the end of the trip. We visited the Garden Tomb, the place Jesus was presumably buried. Although it was a beautiful garden amidst historical artifacts, I found myself unable to connect to the magnitude of the place. When I first walked into the cave, where Jesus is believed to have been laid, a grave calm fell over me. I looked at the stone cave with the prison gate, turned around, and walked right back out. "That's it?" I thought to myself. Feeling disappointed, I decided to give it another try. This time, I saw something that I did not see the first time. There was a wooden sign on the door of the tomb that read, "He is not here - for He is Risen!" When I read those words, it hit me! I had approached the grave of Christ with the same anticipation I would approach a gravesite of a loved one, with remembrance and respect for the dead. This was when the ambiguity I had been experiencing became clear. The reason I was disconnected was because my expectation did not match the Truth. Jesus was not there because He had risen. All of the stories I heard about Jesus had taken on an authentic meaning in my own life. Since that moment I made a decision to choose to believe in the death, burial, and resurrection. Even though I cannot explain it or prove it, I concluded that is what Faith is all about anyway. If I can explain it then there is no need of Faith. So I chose to intentionally direct my Faith toward belief in Jesus Christ, "Son of the Living God".

I tell this story to emphasize the point, in order to speak life we must first believe in the Life that we speak. In America one of the luxuries we have is the ability to choose and construct the message we want to believe. There is no restraint here and unfortunately such has seeped into the delivery of the message of Jesus Christ. I believe the power of the grave speaks more significantly than simply of Jesus raising from the dead. Rather, that it is in the power that was taken out of the hands of the enemy so you and I can live victoriously.

I believe Jesus desires that we search for Him to understand who He is and not rely on a man to convince us of His existence. If we believe all we get from the story of the cross is access into Heaven and an escape from death in eternal destruction, we have only received a portion of the Truth. If we prematurely stop there, we never receive the authority to live as conquerors on Earth. I believe it is a vile disgrace to God's craftsmanship if we only live with thought of the eternal life to come. I believe the elaborate plan of God's masterful design includes the many victories we get to win over Satan in this earthly realm, before we ever make it to Heaven. As believers, we must step into the authoritative role the Father longs for us to firmly grasp here on earth. Today, I challenge you to ask yourself, and answer in Truth, what do you believe?

DEB'S DOWNLOAD

The Cross' victory secured more than eternal salvation, it is also earthly restoration.

MIRROR CHALLENGE

Listen to "Christ is Risen" by Matt Maher

Really ponder the death, burial, and resurrection of Jesus Christ.

1. *Do you believe?*
2. *How can remembering that Jesus is no longer dead help you live Victoriously on earth?*

Write your responses, then read the answers aloud.

STEPS OF PEACE

"Do not fret or have any anxiety about anything, but in every circumstance and in everything, by prayer and petition (definite requests), with thanksgiving, continue to make your wants known to God. And God's peace [shall be yours, that tranquil state of a soul assured of its salvation through Christ, and so fearing nothing from God and being content with its earthly lot of whatever sort that is, that peace] which transcends all understanding shall garrison and mount guard over your hearts and minds in Christ Jesus. For the rest, brethren, whatever is true, whatever is worthy of reverence and is honorable and seemly, whatever is just, whatever is pure, whatever is lovely and lovable, whatever is kind and winsome and gracious, if there is any virtue and excellence, if there is anything worthy of praise, think on and weigh and take account of these things [fix your minds on them."

–Philippians 4:6-8

I have dealt with anxiety my entire life. For as long as I can remember anxiety has consumed every part of me. Everything from trying to please my parents, teacher's expectations, getting A's on assignments, to what guy was going to take me to the prom. It did not help that birth order also played a factor in my learning how to stress. As the second and oldest girl of six children, I was often placed in charge of caring for a younger sibling. The role came with a lot of responsibility and brought a lot of pressure. Even in college, anxiety was too high. I constantly worried about how to please others, make the right grades, or what others thought of me. It is safe to say, that my early years brought many opportunities filled with unnecessary stress. Unknowingly, I had become friends with a major enemy to faith...fear.

As I have learned more about the presence of Faith and its inability to live where there is fear or doubt, the room for anxiety has greatly decreased in my life. Though I do not claim to have arrived to a place of perfection in dealing with overwhelming thoughts; managing the waves of anxiety life brings is getting easier for me. I no longer try to prevent those feelings from entering into my mind and emotions because that is a wasted battle. It's impossible. However, it is possible to apply the four steps listed in Philippians to my life daily and use them, as both a defensive and offensive method, to overcome the stress.

When my mind is being invaded with worries, doubts, and fears about circumstances presently or to come, I pray about it then ask God specifically for what I need. Next, I thank Him because He can do all things and He loves me. Finally, I force myself to think about the positive areas in my life. After completing the steps, not always immediately, but when I continuously apply the principles, the panic begins to subside; then I get to experience what fear never wants me to know...Peace.

No matter what you are facing today, anxiety will only delay your progress. Be intentional about ensuring that Peace is a friend, not its enemy fear.

DEB'S DOWNLOAD

Peace is available to all who practice the steps.

MIRROR CHALLENGE

Practice the steps of Peace

1. *Pray*
2. *Ask*
3. *Give thanks*
4. *Think Positively*

IT'S IN YOUR HANDS

"And let the beauty and delightfulness and favor of the Lord our God be upon us; confirm and establish the work of our hands - yes, the work of our hands, confirm and establish it."

–Psalm 90:17 (AMP)

"BLESSED BE the Lord, my Rock and my keen and firm Strength, Who teaches my hands to war and my fingers to fight."

–Psalm 144:1 (AMP)

I have often heard speakers say, "Don't wait on God to do anything else, because He's not. All that He is going to do, He did it on Calvary." I have never understood the point of that message because it seems so heartless, full of abandonment, and totally not like the character of Jesus...especially my homie Jesus. As a result, I would often dismiss this portion of the sermon. One day while speaking to my brother, Greg, about career opportunities, I said to him, "Maybe, God has allowed you in this space to utilize the creative genius that is inside of you." When those words left my mouth they pierced my heart. For a split second, the work of Jesus being completed those speakers alluded to, actually made sense. After the conversation with my brother, I was forced to apply those often dismissed concepts into my own life.

For the past eight years, an area of internal conflict for me has been extreme discontentment with the types of jobs I have obtained since college. There has been very little personal satisfaction and it seems fulfillment is never attainable. When thinking about my words to my brother I began to consider that maybe God allowed me in this discontented space so I could utilize my own personal genius. I considered what my life would be like if I walked fully in my purpose. So many "what if's" came up. What if I held up my end of the bargain? What if I wrote the book? What if I created the broadcasting network? What if I took the leap into my best self? What if? I realized that my hands needed to get to work.

The Bible tells us that God desires to "bless and establish the work of our hands" and that He "teaches our hands to war and our fingers to fight". Until the conversation with my brother, fighting and war had always been a literal translation to me. One that related to Christ's victory over Satan. Now, fight had taken on an entirely different meaning. The God of Creativity had given me the ability to fight, by building for His Kingdom.

The significant part about these passages are that fight and war allude to struggle and conflict. This is exactly what we will run into when creating. Though not physical, the fight and war is in our ability to stay consistent in Christ and avoid distractions that deter our development. This type of fighting ensures that our hands are free to create the momentum to take us to the next level of our lives.

I believe God desires for us to allow the creativity He gave each of us to run loose into the world so that His Kingdom will get Glory on earth. My friends, in order for this to happen we must allow Him to establish the work so we can build the blessings.

DEB'S DOWNLOAD

Our hands are for more than eating; they were gifted for us to create.

MIRROR CHALLENGE

1. *In what areas are you discontent?*
2. *How can you utilize your hands to create the environment you are seeking?*

Write down the ways for each area then speak your action plan aloud.

Now, get to work and create!

OUT WITH THE OLD, IN WITH THE NEW

"Therefore if any person is [ingrafted] in Christ (the Messiah) he is a new creation (a new creature altogether); the old [previous moral and spiritual condition] has passed away. Behold, the fresh and the new has come!"

–2 Corinthians 5:17

"And no one pours new wine into old wineskins; if he does, the fresh wine will burst the skins and it will be spilled and the skins will be ruined (destroyed). But new wine must be put into fresh wineskins. And no one after drinking old wine immediately desires new wine, for he says, The old is good or better."

–Luke 5:37-39

One of my favorite pastimes is going through old clothes for donation to make room for newer, trendier items. I am not alone in this activity. Every year millions of people turn to their closets for an update and refresh, most commonly on the cuffs of a season cycle. Climate change plays an impactful role in whether clothes should be stored, discarded, or recycled. For example, winter attire does not permit the functionality needed for summer, neither do spring and fall require the same amount of physical coverage. Just as our closets' need to be updated so do our lives. We cannot expect to live productive and fulfilled lives doing the same things for extended periods of time. If we are 50 years old still living the way we did when we were in our 20's there is a strong possibility our lives do not reflect images of our best selves. If we do not learn to identify when change is needed, we will become stagnant and unprepared for what our futures will require of us.

This has not always been a lesson I have understood. Prior to learning the benefit of not hoarding old things, I kept everything because I felt a false obligation to the past. I felt in some way that letting go of an old relationship, friend, job, activity, or way of thinking would leave me destitute and longing for what could have been. However, as I have grown in my ability to walk away and gracefully accept what is to come, I more fully grasp the necessity of achieving this skill set. More importantly, I now see that letting go yields the gift of endless possibilities brewing in the seas of progression.

The first step in creating or experiencing something new is in making a decision. The Bible tells us in 2 Corinthians 5:17 "If any man is in Christ he is a new creation". Before anyone can be in Christ, we must first decide to live a life with Jesus as the head. The new creation does not come until we decide. Just like our wardrobe, it is only when we make the choice to rid ourselves of the old do we become qualified to receive the new. If we try to mix the new way of living under Christ's authority with the old, walking under the influence of Satan, we risk living a life filled with dull living. Let's take the old clothes for example, if we use winter clothes for the summer we will look hot, stuffy, and uncomfortable. This is because there was no adjustment made with the seasonal change.

In Luke 5:37-39 Jesus talks about the process of distributing wine. Back then, if you poured new wine into the old wine partition it would "burst and destroy" the wine. The old skin did not have the capabilities to withstand the elements in the new. If we translate this to life today, trying to accomplish anything we have never had before with outdated methods will destroy our hopes of achieving the dream. Mixing old acquaintances with new purpose-filled relationships more than likely will fail. Starting a business on an employee work ethic will cause frustration and produce little fruit. Building a marriage off of divorced mentorship will probably end terribly. I believe this is because it takes strength and resilience to engage in the unfamiliarly new territories of our lives. Familiarity breeds comfort, which breeds stagnation. If we do not begin to create environments in which our new lives can thrive, we will return to the former ways. I believe it is our duty to remain in Christ who ensures that old things pass away and that we are made new and fresh everyday.

DEB'S DOWNLOAD

The old has reached full capacity. Seek the new.

MIRROR CHALLENGE

Listen to "Clear The Stage" by Jimmy Needham

1. *List the old areas in which you need to embrace new tactics?*
2. *What do you need to decide in order to ensure the new can live?*

Speak the decision list aloud.

Day 6

TRUTHFUL REALITIES

"A time will come, however, indeed it is already here, when the true (genuine) worshipers will worship the Father in spirit and in truth (reality); for the Father is seeking just such people as these as His worshipers. God is a Spirit (a spiritual Being) and those who worship Him must worship Him in spirit and in truth (reality)."

–John 4:23-24

When reading these scriptures the word "truth" forces me to pause. I find it interesting that the Omniscient God of the universe would require us to bring Him the truth when He already knows it. Why would He do this? I believe the answer is found in relationship. Over and over again in the Word, we see how important relationship is to God. Relationship was the cornerstone for Calvary. It was Jesus' bargaining tool to have us reconciled back to the Father. We must not forget, we have agreed to be in partnership with the King of kings. So there is a reason that He qualifies, "true worshipers". Think about it; in our earthly relationships with loved ones and significant others, we do not like it when people are dishonest. So the same goes with God.

This was a difficult concept for me to learn because I did not want to let God down. I figured not telling Him how much I was upset with Him on any given day would be better for the both of us. In actuality, it only hindered our connection. I drew further away from His presence because I was not emptying my soul to Him. What I did not grasp at the time was how imperative integrity is to the worship experience. You see, I now know the intimacy of worship cannot be released into a surface relationship. It takes raw emotions, deep expression of self, and an open vulnerability to be able to fellowship freely in the presence of Jesus.

Now do not get me wrong, it takes much effort to overcome the years of practicing putting on a face for the Faith. It is a huge challenge, one that I do not claim to have mastered. But, my friend, if we ever fully learn how to establish the type of covenant with God that resides in total truth, we will enter into new realms of living. Even greater than that, we will enjoy more secure places of worship with Him. As long as we have on our masks, parading around as someone or something that we are not, we cannot expect anything substantial from God because He cannot bless what we will not bring to Him.

DEB'S DOWNLOAD

Truth allows us to worship in the good of
His presence.

MIRROR CHALLENGE

Ask the Holy Spirit to help you be truthful in your worship to Him.

List ways you will begin to walk in Truth and speak them aloud.

Turn on your favorite worship song.

END IN PRAISE

"Why are you cast down, O my inner self? And why should you moan over me and be disquieted within me? Hope in God and wait expectantly for Him, for I shall yet praise Him, Who is the help of my countenance, and my God."

–Psalm 42:11

In an uninhibited world and culture where nothing is off limits, depression still remains a taboo subject matter. People refuse to talk about it, even less, admit they are suffering with painful emotions, loss of sleep, erratic behavior, and much more. Many times we, Christians, are the least likely to expose that we have moments that seem heavier than we can bear. Not too long ago, I was in my own battle with depression. Honestly, I had been in it longer than I could even remember. The alarming moment I knew it was time for me to get help, was when it began to affect my praise and worship. By the time I reached out to Biblical counselors and spiritual advisors, I was already having suicidal thoughts and losing the ability to function in my daily routine.

As I implemented the resources and fought depression, I realized a lot of Biblical prophets also went through heavy sadness. Quite often, the book of Psalm exhibits first-hand accounts of David in a position of spiritual and emotional unrest. For example, today's scriptural reference depicts clear indicators of David's depression coupled with a spirit of dejection. In spite of the fact that he struggled with persistent episodes of sorrow, David had a unique ability to express himself to God in all situations. He was not afraid to share his fears, weaknesses, or the weight of the path he found himself on at any given time.

In studying, I also found that, even though David was talented at exposing his heart, he was even better at giving God praise. In fact, a highlight of David's character was his ability to turn his depressive cries for help into intentional praise. David always ended by convincing himself in the certainty of the Hope in whom he believed. As I battled, in my own negative space, I gleaned from the wisdom of David and learned how to find a praise to give God in all circumstances.

I believe an indicative attribute of a mature Christian is in our ability to keep a joyful heart and a mouth of praise regardless of the environmental changes we may encounter. Yes, it is important to acknowledge that depression is real and to seek help, if and when, we are feeling especially burdened. Nonetheless, it is more important to acknowledge that we serve a God that never changes, is always with us, and has a plan to get us through every dark place and He deserves our praise.

DEB'S DOWNLOAD

Praise is the balm to heal all wounds.

MIRROR CHALLENGE

Intentionally give God praise by writing down two things that He's protected you from this week.

Call one friend or family member, that you speak to often, and ask how they are doing. Be sure to require an in-depth response.

Reach out to one friend or family member, that you have not spoken to in awhile, and ask them how they are doing. Be sure to wait for a response.

IS GOD ENOUGH?

"For that [Gospel] I am suffering affliction and even wearing chains like a criminal. But the Word of God is not chained or imprisoned! Therefore I [am ready to] persevere and stand my ground with patience and endure everything for the sake of the elect [God's chosen], so that they too may obtain [the] salvation which is in Christ Jesus, with [the reward of] eternal glory."

–2 Timothy 2:9-10

"But DeeDee, can I be enough?"

I was on a plane, leaving Los Angeles headed back to Houston, when I heard what I believe to be the voice of God clearly speak this to me. The words pricked at the tapestry of my heart causing warm tears to stream down my face. As I looked out the window into the emerald-blue Pacific Ocean, I was hurting. There were longings in my heart so deep I could not utter them. Until that moment, I had been attempting to hide those feelings from the all-knowing God. I cried because I knew the appropriate response to the question; however, I also knew that I did not deeply believe God was sufficient enough to fulfill my needs. Instead of answering the painful question, I decided to just feel...the pain.

I felt the emotions of being devastated by my circumstances for the rest of the plane ride home. Later the same night, hesitantly, I began to consider the answer to the question. Before I knew it my emotions were in an upheaval again and I blurted out, "Can you?...You created this void in my heart! You can fill it, but you don't! So I don't know if you can be enough!" Yea, I know, bold stuff to scream to the Creator of the universe, right?

Shortly after my tantrum, I went to sleep. The next morning, I awoke to a surprisingly gentle message from the Holy Spirit, "DeeDee, everything you're concerned about is earthly and temporary. None of it will last. I understand that you want it, but, even when you get it, it won't fulfill the longings that you truly desire. What you are really after is a more intimate relationship with me." Those soft words melted my hard heart. It was then I made a decision. I decided, once and for all, that my answer was, "*Yes*, God is enough for me." Then I picked up my computer to finish this book. I spoke aloud that God was all I needed to complete this work and get it into the hands of many. I believed that with this work I would tour domestically and abroad proclaiming the message of Use Your Words and do my part to help restore the art of communication in the world.

My friend, it is important for us to be aware of the areas we have unintentionally told God, "No, you are not enough." If we never expose these hidden spaces we will never be able to fully embrace the purest form of ourselves or discover our greatest capabilities. Today, I challenge you to sincerely ask yourself, "Is God enough?" Do you really feel that God will satisfy your deepest needs? If you find yourself like me, unable to say yes right away, do not simply give the appropriate response. Allow yourself time to feel and arrive to the truth that will lead you to the Light. Be patient. Wait on Him to bring you to your own yes. When you get there, pattern your life according to the yes. Only remember, your yes requires action.

DEB'S DOWNLOAD

Once you are convinced the Creator of the universe created the universe, you will be confident that He is all you need to do the work He has created for you to complete.

MIRROR CHALLENGE

1. *Refer to your response in Day 5 and ask yourself, "Is God enough?"*

Be truthful in your response. Write down the next steps of your yes.

LOVE TAKES RISK

"Look at the birds of the air; they neither sow nor reap nor gather into barns, and yet your heavenly Father keeps feeding them. Are you not worth much more than they?"

–Matthew 6:26

One song that I loved to hear Whitney Houston sing, was "Jesus Loves Me." Whenever she sang it, you could feel the conviction she felt in those words. Though she struggled with many life battles publicly, I believe she knew Jesus loved her. This is evident in the way she used her God-given talents to accomplish record setting greatness through her music.

Like Whitney, we often sing "Jesus Loves Me", but how many of us truly believe in those words? Does our life showcase the belief that the King of kings loves us? When I first asked myself these questions I had to admit guilt to simply saying words without conviction. I did not really believe Jesus loved me and it was evident. My actions and behaviors resembled those of an orphan fighting to provide for herself. Since God's love for me did not consume my heart, I lived a safe and inhibited lifestyle. Every move I made was calculated by my ability to maintain control of an outcome. I was not living a life filled with a belief that Jesus died on the cross for me to realize my maximum potential.

As I journeyed through self-actualization and recognizing my need to be filled with God's love, I concluded that if I truly believed God loved me I would take more risks. I would be more vulnerable or even give more of my material belongings without thought of when I would receive a return. I began to take greater steps of faith in my life. I no longer depended on my own wallet, merit, or degrees to qualify me for my purpose. Instead, I accepted Christ's love for me. In doing so, I received freedom to move confidently toward my dreams because I not only believed, I knew He had my back.

For a moment, consider the characteristics of the "birds of the air" discussed in Matthew 6. Birds are wild and free creatures. When they leave their nests they do not typically return. They rely completely on the provision of Christ to supply their every need. As the scriptures probe, how much more valuable are we to God than a bird? Yet, how much more stagnate can we find humans than our avian friends? I further pondered on how birds use their wings to fly. They do not concern themselves with the wind needed to ensure they stay in flight, they just do what they were created to do. I believe God wants us to live like free birds. No concern for how things will happen, only trusting they will happen. I believe He wants us to rest confidently in the love He has for us and be an example to others by the way we boldly live our lives.

DEB'S DOWNLOAD

Believing in Him gives life. Believing in His Love changes life.

MIRROR CHALLENGE

Repeat the phrase, "God loves me, Jesus died for me, the Holy Spirit cares for me." (3x times)

Write down what it means for you to be loved by the Father, Son, & Holy Spirit; individually and collectively.

1. *Consider the birds. What does flying look like in your life? What faith-risks could you take that would require you to depend on -God and not yourself?*

YOU ARE SPECIAL

"For You did form my inward parts; You did knit me together in my mother's womb. I will confess and praise You for You are fearful and wonderful and for the awful wonder of my birth! Wonderful are Your works, and that my inner self knows right well."

–Psalm 139:13-14

There is a quote by Kathryn Stockett, author of *The Help*, that says, "You is kind. You is smart. You is important." This quote first became famous when the novel became a blockbuster film in 2011. It has been widely used as satire, locally and even nationally, on various media outlets. Although it has been the center of lots of laughter, I have often worried if the core of its message was being overlooked.

We, the human race, are special not just in God's eyes, but in the unique gift we have to connect, engage, procreate, and coexist with one another. We are special because we do not have to walk on four legs or swim in an ocean to live. We are special because we have a brain to think and decipher information instead of depending on another earthly being to take care of our every need. We are special to have been chosen amongst millions of sperm cells to live. All too often we miss the basic importance of that truth by blending into the cultural norm.

Being special does not mean that everyone will be able to grasp the degree and depth of your independent value and beauty; thankfully, that is not what matters. My friend, what is vital is that we acquire that knowledge then pursue life from that solid foundation.

DEB'S DOWNLOAD

Your unique specialty is the door to your craft.

MIRROR CHALLENGE

Identify three different ways that you are special.

Text those ways to yourself.

Now, while looking directly in the mirror, speak those ways to yourself aloud.

Day 11

PRESS PLAY

"But no weapon that is formed against you shall prosper, and every tongue that shall rise against you in judgement you shall show to be in the wrong. This [peace, righteousness, security, triumph over opposition] is the heritage of the servants of the Lord [those in whom the ideal Servant of the Lord is reproduced]; this is the righteousness or the vindication which they obtain from Me [this is that which I impart to them as their justification], says the Lord."

–Isaiah 54:17

Growing up in the 90's, Nintendo and Sega Genesis game consoles were very popular. These consoles were often the center of many sibling feuds in our household. When playing, it was inevitable that a loser would emerge from the battle. Often when this happened, the losing player would press the pause button on their controller in order to slow the imminent winner's momentum from advancing to the finish line. This was a way to frustrate the organic process of the game. In life we can find ourselves in similar situations. It looks as if things are going well then for an eventful twist, there is an unexpected delay.

In 2015, I found myself in this type of game experience, only it was real life. It seemed pause had been pressed on every ambitious bone in my body. As a result, my thoughts became defeated and I lived in a constant state of un-fulfillment, humiliation, and discontentment. Comparing my life to others, nothing seemed fair and I was frustrated with the way things were working out for me. Unconsciously, I became the victim in my own story and stopped doing the things I loved. One day after growing tired of what I had become, I recalled the scenarios of playing games as a child. Whether we had to wrestle and fight one another, or call our parents to help settle the score, we never allowed the game to stay paused for long. No matter what, the priority was to press play and get the game started again. So I decided to apply those same principles and get the game started back in my own life. Consequently, I began to enjoy life again. Over time, exercising, hanging with family and friends, and reactivating my business, "Use Your Words The Movement" became pleasures once more.

Make no mistake my friend, challenges are inevitable. In life, Satan will bring unquestionable amounts of resistance in an attempt to block and hinder our progress. The good news is, he cannot stop us from winning. Only we can stop ourselves from advancing by allowing our lives to stay paused. It is important to remember, regardless of what comes to stop us, we have a controller too. We have to press play and finish the race of our lives. We do this by utilizing the resources available to us through prayer and scripture, gathering information from mentors and getting active working toward a more positive future. I encourage you today, do not allow life to pause you in the middle of the game. Press play and finish the course. Only then can we go to the next level.

DEB'S DOWNLOAD

Those who fight to play, win the game.

MIRROR CHALLENGE

Consider the game of life...

1. *Are you paused? If so, write down the ways.*
2. *Are you playing? If so, give concrete evidence proving such.*

If you are paused, list at least three things you can do to unpause your life then speak them aloud.

THE GRIND OF FAITH

I have fought the good (worthy, honorable, and noble) fight, I have finished the race, I have kept (firmly held) the faith. [As to what remains] henceforth there is laid up for me the [victor's] crown of righteousness [for being right with God and doing right], which the Lord, the righteous Judge, will award to me and recompense me on that [great] day–and not to me only, but also to all those who have loved and yearned for and welcomed His appearing (His return).

–2 Timothy 4:7-8

As we are on our journeys of believing and building, it is perfectly normal to feel the devastation of defeat. There will be times when every step forward forms cracks that spread to create a divide between the life you have and the one you have imagined. It is during these moments that isolation can be magnified, but it is important to remember that this is life. There is nothing wrong with you. Actually, very few are even afforded the pain of this uncertainty, because few challenge the status quo to pursue their greatest potential. I want you to know today that you are fine just the way you are. Keep going, step by step, you will build what you see, if you do not quit. The only way to fail is to turn the opposite direction of the resistance. Be strategic, get a plan, then follow through because "the race is not to the swift".

I am realizing that God places us in situations that seemingly have nothing to do with our dreams or destiny. It is in these times that we must embrace the process and trust the processor to complete us, the processed. He will make us ready and equipped for what the dream or destination will require of us. This in fact will require a state of maturity that makes us willing to endure the tribulation, fatigue, and apathy that come with brewing success. This does not mean that God is mad at us and no our lives are not unfair. It is all a process.

Today, Lord I ask that you would keep me and my friend in perfect peace as we keep our minds focused on you. In a life where fame can come through media uploads, stories can be told in fifteen seconds, and the number of likes depicts the integrity of a brand, it can be hard to remember that firm foundations take time to create. Help us God to have patience and perseverance and let us not become too tired to work and finish what we started. In Jesus' Name, Amen.

DEB'S DOWNLOAD

Endure.

MIRROR CHALLENGE

Listen to "Our God Is Greater" by Chris Tomlin

Investigate yourself. Name the areas you need to endure.

1. *What does endurance look like?*
2. *Do you believe that God is greater and that His plan is better?*

STRENGTH IN WEAKNESS

"So for the sake of Christ, I am well pleased and take pleasure in infirmities, insults, hardships, persecutions, perplexities and distresses; for when I am weak [in human strength], then am I [truly] strong (able, powerful in divine strength)."
–2 Corinthians 12:10

In life there are times when we feel like we have given all that we have to offer. Moments when frustration gets the best of us and even when sickness interrupts our lives. During these weak moments, it is important to stop and acknowledge that we need the strength of a Being far greater than ourselves. Many times we cover all of the bases alone. We forfeit help, then overexert our strength. I believe it was moments like these in which Paul referred. He understood the importance of knowing that true help comes from God.

So what does that mean for us? I believe it means that we have to take a moment to acknowledge that in our humanness we are flawed and are not capable of being strong all of the time. We have to ask God's Holy Spirit for wisdom, guidance, and help. Then we get to watch how productivity becomes accessible. I have had to learn this immensely when writing this book. There were days when I physically did not feel well yet I had to write. I would pray and ask the Holy Spirit to give me the words that someone needed to uplift their spirit...and my own. When I focused on His strength, not my weakness, I was amazed by how the words would fill my mind and these pages.

Father, today I pray you would slow my friends and I down. I pray we see that we do not have to carry the burden of this task you have asked us to complete. Lord you delight in watching us grow down here on Earth; so I am asking you to fill my friends and I with a heart to ask you for help. In a society that promotes individuality and independence, it can be really hard to focus on depending solely on you, especially because you are invisible. Lord help us to comprehend the necessity of being completely transparent with you. Father, fill us and complete us by your perfect strength which is found in your joy. In Jesus' name, I pray, Amen.

DEB'S DOWNLOAD

Our weakness should bring us to His strength.

MIRROR CHALLENGE

1. *In what areas are you trying to carry the burden alone?*

Ask God for help in those areas aloud.

THE GOD OF RESTORATION, RENEWAL, AND PEACE

"Peace I leave with you; My [own] peace I now give and bequeath to you. Not as the world gives do I give to you. Do not let your hearts be troubled, neither let them be afraid. [Stop allowing yourselves to be agitated and disturbed; and do not permit yourselves to be fearful and intimidated and cowardly and unsettled.]"

–John 14:27

"The law of the Lord is perfect, restoring the [whole] person; the testimony of the Lord is sure, making wise the simple."

–Psalm 19:7

As I have mentioned in earlier chapters, I have suffered from anxiety most of my life. In times past, I have mistakenly assumed everyone deals with the chaotic angst associated with the emotional disorder. Out of my five siblings, my youngest brother, Mykhael, happens to be one of those low-to-no anxiety people. Over the years he has taught me a lot about controlling my stress levels. Probably the most laid back person you will ever meet, the man lets everything roll right off of his 6'4" back. I have to be honest, it drives me crazy to watch him live so peacefully.

One day while he and I were talking (I was probably in the middle of an anxiety attack) he said to me, "DeeDee why do you care so much? I learned a long time ago what I can control and I deal with that, what I cannot I just say, ok." As he shrugged his shoulders, he went on to explain how it was to my own advantage to learn to let things be, because others are not going to stress out as much as I am; therefore, it is no use in driving myself crazy. I have never forgotten that conversation. Now I would like to say that Mykhael and I have only had that type of conversation once and I immediately changed my way of living, but then I would be lying. It has been a process. Because the unstable emotions were so integrated within me, I never thought I could be healed or know a life without anxiety.

A while ago I decided to seek out Biblical resources to help me in my process of healing. In my studies I noticed two things about anxiety. First, for me, it is a learned behavior and not apart of my true, authentic self. Scripture often reveals God's generous gift of Peace. Jesus says in John 14:27, "Peace I leave with you; My peace." This means just as there is opportunity to take on anxiety which comes from Satan, there is also a choice to choose Peace, which comes from Christ. The same passage in John further suggests that we have the power to "stop allowing yourselves to be agitated and disturbed; and do not permit yourselves to be fearful and intimidated and cowardly and unsettled." Secondly, I learned that even though stress and anxiety take a toll on my physical body, I can be healed from its effects. In other words, God takes delight in restoring me and my nervous system. Psalm 19:7 says, "The law of the Lord is perfect, restoring the [whole] person." Isn't it great to know that no matter what life has tried to put on us, we do not have to stay that way?

Today, I challenge you to search your heart and ask God to help you fill the areas in which you need to be restored. Remember that restoration takes time. However, if you are patient and consistent, you and God will have a great chance of revealing to the world what His original plan was when He created you.

DEB'S DOWNLOAD

In a world full of choices, choose restoration and peace.

MIRROR CHALLENGE

Listen to "My Heart Has Been Restored" by Maurette Brown Clark.

1. *Refer to Day 3; have you been applying the steps?*
2. *What areas in your life need to be restored from anxiety?*

Write down at least two areas. Now, ask God for help to be renewed.

GLIMPSES OF YESTERDAY

"When I was a child, I talked like a child, I thought like a child, I reasoned like a child; now that I have become a man, I am done with childish ways and have put them aside."

–1 Corinthians 13:11

This verse has always been one of my favorite Scriptures. With such a straightforward message, it leaves little room for confusion or misunderstanding. One of the many reasons I love this passage is because of its emphasis on self-development. Using the past as a gauge, to measure growth in the present, is a vital key toward the bettering of self. Once, during a time of reflection I wrote a letter to my younger self that read:

> 10 years ago she was scared and brave. She knew there was a future she'd never seen waiting to be possessed. If I could tell this young girl something, I'd say...'You're a force and a light of passion. Don't underestimate the power of your influence because your presence is great and it matters!' Never would this little girl have imagined then that she would have lived the life that she's lived so far. There's so much more life to consume, but as of now I'm happy with what she's done, who she's become, and the impact she's made. Maya Angelou once said, 'People will forget what you said, people will forget what you did, but they will never forget how you made them feel.' To this young girl, I say 'Thank you!', You've validated my purpose of existence and you've tested the borders of my surroundings. I'm grateful for your talent and ambition. Keep going forward.

I wrote this letter while looking at my high school senior portrait and was surprised at the stream of tears that began to fall down my eyes. For one moment I was not being hard on myself or calculating all the things I had not done. Instead I acknowledged that the journey was indeed filled with mistakes and shortcomings but also successes and accomplishments. I share this with you not to boast, but to remind you to do the same. In our social media world it is easy to fall prey to the trap of comparison. In doing so, we neglect to celebrate the journey we have taken and the growth that comes with it.

Though, never good to set up camp, it is important for us to use the past as a tool for growth instead of a pool of shame. Though we all have things in our childhood or past that we may not be proud of, the fact that it is in the past suggests that we have access to a brighter future.

Father, I ask that you help me and my friend to be better lovers of self, though, not in vanity or in a way that exalts ourselves above you. I pray that we learn to love ourselves as you desire we love our neighbors. It is in Jesus' name I pray,

Amen.

DEB'S DOWNLOAD

A true mark of maturity is how well you leave your past.

MIRROR CHALLENGE

Write a letter to your 10 year younger self. Be kind, truthful, and transparent. Use this as a time to make peace with any shortcomings and be sure to give praise for the progress you have made. Then, while standing in the mirror, read the letter aloud.

PURGE

"Cast your burden on the Lord [releasing the weight of it] and He will sustain you; He will never allow the [consistently] righteous to be moved (made to slip, fall, or fail)."

–Psalm 55:22

I am a gadget girl. At any given time I will have my Macbook Pro alongside my Mac Air, which will be charging my iPad mini, while holding a FaceTime conversation on my latest iPhone. My bend toward electronics started when I was a kid. My first electronic toys were a portable cassette walkman and a polaroid camera. Since then, the world of technology has evolved immensely. One of the greatest changes is in the way we store information. We used to backup our information on floppy discs or jump drives. Now there is iCloud, Dropbox, and other online storage services.

Ever so often, when using a technology device, applications begin to freeze. This is often followed by a "storage full" notification. When this happens I make a trip to the Genius bar, Geek Squad, or whatever other 'nerd' team that will assist me. There job is to help me safely backup my information into iCloud or on my external hard drive. This process includes updating software and wiping the data off all devices. Once the software update has been completed there are two options: first, restore from backup, which adds all old information back onto the device, or setup as new. Most often I opt for the second option because I am a hoarder of pictures and text messages. And it is all fun and games until they become the culprits behind the nagging "storage full" messages.

As I grow I am learning that we humans do the same thing with our minds. For years and years we are filled with moments and memories, negative and positive thoughts, accusations and rebuttals. We hold onto so many things without stopping to purge our spiritual, mental, and even physical systems. Failing to eliminate the unnecessary waste is detrimental to the longevity of our lives. It creates stress and causes us to freeze and crash, just as do our electronic devices.

When God created us, He modeled each of one with a specific capacity restraint. We are not designed to hold all of the pressure life brings. This can be from our own expectations, family members, employers, or even peers. We are just not equipped for it. Yet, we often find ourselves right smack in the middle of a "storage full" moment. In these times we have to purge ourselves properly. Psalm 55:22 tells us exactly how to do this by "casting your burdens on the Lord". When we take time to purge ourselves, we are creating an ability for more productivity.

We renew our minds to be able to sustain longer, just as when I purge my technology devices more workspace is created and their lifespans are lengthened. If we fully expect to reach our maximum potential, it is important we learn to acknowledge the "storage full" notifications our bodies and minds receive. To reach our optimum utilization, we must refrain from overloading our systems.

DEB'S DOWNLOAD

Avoid the crash. Purge.

MIRROR CHALLENGE

1. *In which areas are your "storage full"?*
2. *How can you begin to purge?*

Begin the purge by telling an accountability partner your action plan.

DARK PLACES

"Things are hidden temporarily only as a means to revelation.] For there is nothing hidden except to be revealed, nor is anything [temporarily] kept secret except in order that it may be known."

–Mark 4:22

"Pride goes before destruction, and a haughty spirit before a fall."

–Proverbs 16:18

We have all heard stories of people who have risen to the top of their career field; doing great things for their communities, winning awards, and becoming champions in their craft. All of this only to find in the end, these same people lived with secrets dark enough to override every accomplishment. Stories like these tarnish the sanctity of a life filled with positive work by leaving legacies of dishonesty and families to deal with the shame of the irresponsible actions. Though, having less than satisfactory areas in our lives is to be expected simply by being amongst the human condition. When we entered into this world, we came into a broken, hurting place filled with destructiveness. For most, it is hard to accept that at our core we have the capacity to be mischievous, vile, and deceptive creatures. Fortunately, because of the work of Jesus we have an opportunity to conquer these negative spaces before they conquer us.

A dark place is the area in your life that you intentionally have to overcome in order to function at your prime. For example, one of my dark areas is anger. I have had to work forcibly to manage my temperament. Over the years it has become much better than it once was; however, it is only because of the steps taken to manage the behavior am I now more in control. The first step in dealing with dark places is acknowledging it exists. I had to admit it was not normal to be as internally frustrated as I would become in situations that should not warrant an angry response. I was having abnormal emotions to normal situations. Secondly, I had to seek counsel. I met with mentors and told them about my issues. These were people that I trusted not to share my information carelessly and who would pray with, and for me, and help me to get the resources I needed to get better. These types of influencers can also be a pastor, psychologist, counselor, friend, or confidant.

Dark places can be difficult to talk about but it is necessary. If we ever expect to reach our greatest potential in life we have to be aware, almost acquaintances, with our dark places. By "acquaintances" I mean, do not suppress or act like your dark place does not exist. The most important key is not to be so prideful to think you can handle your dark place alone. Unfortunately, that is the reason we hear so many triumphant stories turn into tragedy. If dark places are not managed appropriately Light will one day find its way into your darkness and present it center stage. I pray that is not our story.

DEB'S DOWNLOAD

Deal with the dark, but stay in the Light.

MIRROR CHALLENGE

Admit & Seek

Admit your dark places.

Write them down and make a plan of action to deal with them.

Seek someone you trust to share this information with so you do not walk alone.

NEW THINGS

"Do not [earnestly] remember the former things; neither consider the things of old. Behold, I am doing a new thing! Now it springs forth; do you not perceive and know it and will you not give heed to it? I will even make a way in the wilderness and rivers in the desert."

–Isaiah 43:18-19

I am thoroughly accustomed (almost addicted) to change and new beginnings, a quality I enjoy most about myself. Whether it be traveling to a new city, eating at a new restaurant, purchasing a unique shoe, or testing a new hairstyle, I love change and embrace it every chance that I get. At the age of 23, I was taking ballet class with grade school children. At 24, I left my job in Mississippi and moved to Los Angeles. At 25 I shaved my head bald. Two months later I bleached the newly grown hair platinum blonde. At 27 I got Invisalign for my teeth. At 28 I enrolled in swimming lessons. At 29 I moved from Houston back to my home state of Mississippi, to Connecticut, then to New York all in seven months. I have moved across the country three times in six years and have been a citizen in 3 different states. Change, for me, has been the incubator that breeds the passion I have for life.

Although change has become my friend, I have not always welcomed the adjustments as gracefully. I had to learn to adapt at the rate of change in my life. Though, change is the only constant in life, I am always surprised by the comments I receive about my level of openness. "Deborah is so crazy", "Deborah is always doing something", "Where the heck are you?", are comments and questions I often hear. In times of old, I would take offense or attempt to suppress my desires for adventure to fit into the environment in which I found myself. For a large part of my life I concluded that something was wrong with me, that I was running away from stability. More recently, I have found the courage to accept these attributes about myself as the stamp that makes me priceless.

I remember when I got Invisalign and decided to close the diastema between my front teeth. When I told my mom she said to me, "Well, bye Deborah, we're sure going to miss you." So often this is the way we view change. As if what has been is greater than what can ever be. Meanwhile, we expect that which is to come will be a more painful, intolerable experience. Why do we forfeit excitement when plunging into the unknown? Is it because we lack the understanding of Who goes with us? Think about the skies, no two days are the same. God, in all of His majesty, ensured that we are able to witness the eclectic variations of His artwork on a daily basis. Now, if God cares enough about the sky showcasing an ever-changing dynamic, He surely cares if we are living a life filled with variety and passion. As I grow more into the personality that God intended for me, I bask in the part of me that does not flinch when asked to dye my hair blonde or travel out of the country without familiar faces to accompany me. I would like to think it is in these times I bleed the DNA of God most. I believe God takes delight when we live life without reservation and embrace endless possibilities through Him.

What about you? Everyone's story will not be the same, but when is the last time you have tried something new? Have you become so accustomed to your schedule that you live your life without thought because it is all planned out? Have you become so well trained in your habits that the dog knows your routine? Don't get me wrong here, there is nothing wrong with having structure, however, I believe a major part of growing into our fullest potential is in our ability to expand our borders and stretch the horizons of our comfort zones. I strongly believe that predictability is a key to falling into a slump which can invite depression if not careful.

Today, I challenge you to be creative and invent a new way to do an old thing. Instead of taking the same path to work, go an alternate route. Try making a new recipe for dinner. It is in the small things that we see the hand of God guiding us to the lives we have hoped to live. God wants us to experience new things on a daily basis, not just on special occasions. Engage in the zest of life today, your life awaits!

DEB'S DOWNLOAD

Change is the match that ignites the fires of life.

MIRROR CHALLENGE

Consider how you view change.

1. *When is the last time you have done something new?*
2. *How can you incorporate a new change into your life today?*

Text 3 ways to yourself, then do them.

FOCUS ON THE HAPPY

"For David says in regard to Him, I saw the Lord constantly before me, for He is at my right hand that I may not be shaken or overthrown or cast down [from my secure and happy state]. Therefore my heart rejoiced and my tongue exulted exceedingly; moreover, my flesh also will dwell in hope [will encamp, pitch its tent, and dwell in hope in anticipation of the resurrection]."

–Acts 2:25-26

Growing up, two of my favorite movies were "Polly" and "Pollyanna". These movies were adapted from the novel, Pollyanna, written by Eleanor H. Porter in 1913. The story line for the Pollyanna franchise is based on a young orphan girl sent to live with her wretched aunt in a downtrodden town. Pollyanna, a high-spirited, positive ball of energy is known for playing "The Glad Game". She was taught this game by her father, who used it as a way to find the good in every situation. Eventually Pollyanna would spread her positivity to everyone throughout the town and uplift their spirits, even angry Aunt Polly. What I loved most about the storyline of both movies was how good I felt when it ended. Afterwards, I would even play my own "Glad Game".

Throughout life we have been told happiness is a choice and our ability to be happy should not be dependent upon what is happening to us, but on our decision to be in control of our emotions in any given state. I never understood how we, unlike Pollyanna, who would eventually end up getting into a devastating accident leaving her paralyzed, have the power to choose our response to life's circumstances. I thought that I must feel happy in order to have the power to be happy. Boy! I could not have been more wrong in that assumption. As I have grown, I now understand it is my responsibility to choose where my emotions will live. That in fact, no event or person has the power to alter my mood unless I hand them the authority to do so.

As I grow more rooted and secure in my relationship in Christ, I have a better understanding that He is my constant. Life will change at any moment, but as long as I am in the right relationship with Him, my Joy will be found in Him. I love Acts 2:25, "....for He is at my right hand that I may not be shaken or overthrown or cast down [from my secure and happy state]." It is in our power, because only we have the authority to determine what will be our focus. If we choose to focus on the negative or less desirable situation then we will experience negative and less than desirable feelings. However, if we maturely place our thoughts on the fact that Jesus is right beside us and the Holy Spirit is present to help us, then we are acting in our power and our right to live in the "secure and happy state". A state not based on emotions, rather on the decision to live our best life.

DEB'S DOWNLOAD

Exercise your rights! It is within our right to be happy.

MIRROR CHALLENGE

Play "The Glad Game"

1. *How can you choose to be glad about the less favorable situations in your life?*

Write at least 5 ways down then speak them aloud.

FREE THE POWER

"As each of you has received a gift (a particular spiritual talent, a gracious divine endowment), employ it for one another as [befits] good trustees of God's many-sided grace [faithful stewards of the extremely diverse powers and gifts granted to Christians by unmerited favor]."

–1 Peter 4:10

"Freeing the power of the individual." I always loved the mission of my beloved alma mater, The University of Southern Mississippi. This quote made an impact on my life because it acknowledged the individuality in each student on the campus. Though we were a collective whole, the power lay in our own creative uniqueness. To me, "freeing" suggested a process of obtaining power. Naturally, the university's message pointed toward the completion of a degree; however, the meaning resonated much further than higher education. Surprisingly, it crept into the realm of my purpose.

For many years the abstract reason of my existence loomed greatly over me. Often I would question why I was born to earth. Over time I have found the answer to be communication. In hindsight the answer would not have been so difficult to find had I paid closer attention to the areas of my giftings. As a child talking and writing were my strong points. However, I grew up in a small town in Mississippi that did not cultivate creativity, so there were not ample opportunities to foster those gifts. Though it took time, as I grew in the development of my creativity, my purpose in communication began to be distributed through the means of ministry and motivation and resulted in my online business. It is interesting to note, it was not until I understood my own gifts did I receive the power. When the power did finally come, freedom reigned in my ability to accomplish my purpose more easily.

When our gifts are utilized to benefit our purpose, power is released from Heaven. This power ignites a passion to aide us in completing the work we have been called to fulfill. Thereby, beautifully showcasing the magnificent mission of my alma mater. When God created us, it was with a specific purpose to be completed. He did not bring us to earth without help to succeed. As a loving parent, He placed the gifts and tools we would need to accomplish our purpose on the inside of us.

DEB'S DOWNLOAD

Our gifts unlock the power.

MIRROR CHALLENGE

1. *What are your gifts? Write them down.*
2. *Do you know your purpose? Write it down.*

Pray and ask God to help you understand how He intended for your gifts to be used toward your purpose.

MOMENTS THAT MATTER

"Iron sharpens iron; so a man sharpens the countenance of his friend [to show rage or worthy purpose]."

–Proverbs 27:17

1980's hip hop group, Whodini, had a famous song called, "Friends". The chorus' lyrics say, "Friends. How many of us have them? Friends. One's we can depend on?" The importance of the message is relevant still today. The intent of friendship is that we learn to build together and engage with others and not live life alone. Unfortunately, today's society prides itself on being independent and needs, as rapper Drake would say, "no new friends". I believe statements such as "no new friends" exist from the baggage of past hurts and betrayal. Because we live in a time when most seek the benefit of self, it has become increasingly difficult to allow new relationships to form. Taking on this type of mindset invades our communities with seeds of distrust and creates homes of isolation.

For as long as I can remember, friendships have been the foundation of most of my prayer requests. In grade school, middle school, and all through high school I never felt like I fit into the crowd. As I have gained clarity on what true friendship is, I now understand that a lot of the relationships I wanted were not based on authenticity, but rather on fleeting circumstances. Back then I wanted friends to go to the mall, have sleepovers, and talk about girly things. Though, these are activities we share with friends, the core of a friendship does not require them. I now understand that I do not need friends to go to the mall, though it is nice. What I *need* in friendship is someone praying for me to overcome obstacles and cheering me along to fulfill my purpose and destiny, and I for them.

A true friend is concerned about the way you live your life and pushes you to be the best version of yourself. Genuine friends have the ability and capacity to see the friendship through the bumps and bruises of traveling along the road of purpose. It is to our own advantage to take notice of our friendships and cultivate them. We have to be open to receive new relationships, not too stubborn to let go of the toxic ones, and responsible enough to care to sharpen, and be sharpened, by those in which we open our lives.

DEB'S DOWNLOAD

Be friends on purpose.

MIRROR CHALLENGE

Confront yourself.

1. *Identify your true friends. Write them down.*
2. *How sincere of a friend have you been to them lately?*
3. *Are these friends giving, taking, or both from the relationship? What about you?*

Call/Text your true friends and tell them "Thank you for being a friend."

BELIEVE IN THE WORK YOU DO

"And out of the ground the Lord God formed every [wild] beast and living creature of the field and every bird of the air and brought them to Adam to see what he would call them; and whatever Adam called every living creature, that was its name. And Adam gave names to all the livestock and to the birds of the air and to every [wild] beast of the field..."

–Genesis 2:19-20a

Wow! Can you imagine this astounding image? Adam was given the task of naming every "beast and living creature" on earth. When I first read this text, the fact that God brought the animals to see what Adam would call them stood out to me. He knew that He built Adam with the capabilities and creativity to fulfill the task! Isn't that exciting? It speaks to the confidence God has in the things He creates. Not only is God the creator of the animals, He is the creator of Adam.

Now consider this. What if Adam said, "Oh no God! I can't do this, I don't even know what those things are, you created them so you do it!" I wonder what would have happened? Since God purposed Adam to name the creatures and He, Himself, only intended to create them, I wonder if the task would have been left incomplete? Thankfully, Adam did not miss the opportunity to make a lasting impact on mankind by stepping into the freedom of His God-given gifts and creating with authority. The Scripture says, "...and whatever Adam called every living creature, that was its name." The God of the universe put Adam in charge, and Adam did not disappoint. What an awe-inspiring example for us today!

Like Adam, God has created countless tasks for each of us on earth to complete. Not one of us are here without a heavenly assignment. When God presents us with this task, called purpose; it is not for us to fight against it, talk back to God like He chose the wrong person, or get started when we feel like it. No, in this moment, we are to step up and do what we have been called to do. We have to believe, like Adam, that God would not ask us to do anything He has not already equipped us for. Let's think about Adam for a moment. As far as we know Scripturally, this is the first time he has spoken. Therefore, his vocabulary could not have been advanced. Adam was faced with the daunting undertaking of individually naming the entire lexicon of the animal kingdom, without having ever spoken a word prior. In spite of that, he did it. Doesn't this sound like the character of God? Instead of asking us to fulfill things within our comfort zone or an area in which we are adequately experienced, He places us where we are least qualified. This is so that He can get the glory.

In times past, when I have found myself in similar situations, I cannot say that I was as obedient as Adam to complete my own task. Unlike Adam, I did not believe in my ability to complete my work. I believed in God and that He could do it, but I was not confident in the abilities that God had given to me. Belief is such a key element in the execution process as we begin to work toward our goals. If we do not believe in ourselves then it is unimaginable to hope others will do the same. Our belief must be greater than our doubt, it is like a muscle. It has to be stretched and developed so that its external results can manifest.

As I gain more belief, I am finding that developed belief breeds confidence. I am growing more confident in myself as well as God's capabilities to perform His great works in and through my life. There is confidence in being able to ask God for anything I need and peace knowing that I am working with Him, and not against Him. Though absolutely imperative, our confidence cannot only be found in God. We must also have confidence in what He put inside of us as well. Like Adam, we have to walk confidently in the authority that God has given each of us to carry out our purpose.

DEB'S DOWNLOAD

Strengthen your belief then do what He has called you to do.

MIRROR CHALLENGE

Consider Adam then refer back to your answers for Day 10 & 11

1. *Have you "unpaused" your "gifts"?*
2. *Reread your list aloud. Comparing to today's topic has it changed any?*

PROTECT THE GIFTS

"Jacob was boiling pottage (lentil stew) one day, when Esau came from the field and was faint [with hunger]. And Esau said to Jacob, I beg of you, let me have some of that red lentil stew to eat, for I am faint and famished! That is why his name was called Edom [red]. Jacob answered, Then sell me today your birthright (the rights of a firstborn). Esau said, See here, I am at the point of death; what good can this birthright do me? Jacob said, Swear to me today [that you are selling it to me]; and he swore to [Jacob] and sold him his birthright."

–Genesis 25:29-33

Have you ever felt overlooked? Perhaps you have wondered if anyone cares about you or even thinks about your well being. If you are like me these thoughts of self-pity can easily come into our minds, cause frustration, and alter our emotions. The purpose of these thoughts are to distract us from the greater purpose of our lives. If we are feeling bad, there is a great chance that we will not be as eager to answer the call to accomplish our goals. One day when I was experiencing this I heard the Holy Spirit say to me, "Writing is a gift I gave you; don't allow Satan to steal your gift." At the time I was allowing so many excuses to prevent me from writing. When I heard this, immediately the story of Esau and Jacob came to mind. In that story, Esau allowed his brother, Jacob, to trick him out of his birthrights because he had not placed enough value on his own gifts. Esau sold Jacob his birth order rights essentially for a bowl of soup because he was hungry. Can you imagine? His entire life's worth traded for one meal.

I used to feel sorry for Esau and would get angry with God. I did not believe that He should have allowed Jacob to get away with his deceptive plot. Now, I see that God is blameless and I am able to remove some of the blame from Jacob and properly place considerable responsibility on Esau. Esau was the first born, it was his duty to himself to ensure that he received his inheritance from his father. Because he did not, we now see the results of not protecting our gifts.

To bring it home, as a writer, a few of my responsibilities are to sharpen my craft through studying the rules of grammar, writing daily, reading to increase my vocabulary and reading speed, and understanding literary content. It is no one else's responsibility to ensure that I can reach my goals with my gifts and talents but my own. I have to gauge what I watch and what goes into my mind so that I do not contaminate the words and visions that enhance my creativity. As I pondered on how this story related to my own life, I realized that in many ways Satan is like Jacob. He sees that we have something of value and his plan is to disrupt us from receiving all that God has for us. Prior to hearing the Holy Spirit say "don't let Satan steal your gift," I had never really thought about my ability to write as something special or of value, much less something that I needed to protect. The day I heard the Holy Spirit changed the way I view myself and the blessings God has given to me. I began to understand the responsibility I have in ensuring that I reach the pinnacle of where my gifts will take me.

Like Esau, there is an enemy that wants to prevent us from obtaining our spiritual inheritance. However, if we stay in position and mentally prepared for any of his tactics, we can remain stable enough to access what is rightfully ours. Today, I challenge you to drop the distractions, and take responsibility for your own gifts, lest you leave them dormant for Satan to "steal, kill, and destroy". So, own it with care.

DEB'S DOWNLOAD

Don't be fooled. Protect your gift.

MIRROR CHALLENGE

Refer to Day 20 Mirror Challenge.

1. *Are you being a good protector of your gifts? If so, how?*
2. *How can you better protect the gifts God has given you?*

THE REQUIREMENT OF WORSHIP

"Then Abraham said to his servants, Settle down and stay here with the donkey, and I and the young man will go yonder and worship and come again to you."
–Genesis 22:5

Worship. Worship. Worship. Oh how sweet the sound of an authentic worship to King Jesus. In a broken world filled with pain, flawed humans, and corrupt societies, worship helps us escape the presence of wickedness here on earth. Worship is designed that we might create a space for God's presence to dwell without interruption. It is a gift we give ourselves to break free from the chains of depression, discouragement, doubt, fear, anxiety, and worry. Worship obliterates Satan's attempts to block our relationship with the Father, God. In a sense, worship is a weapon. Somehow in our culture, we have confused worship as something that is primarily done when life is flowing smoothly and when all of our prayers have been answered. Mistakenly, we have formulated that worship equates to perfect living. In error, we often wait for the manifestation of a miracle to offer God a sacrifice of praise and worship.

In the Bible, the very first time worship is documented is in the context of an imminent death. Isaac, Abraham's promised son, is to be sacrificed as an act of obedience to God. I believe Abraham understood, though His situation did not yield a zealous emotion, he was required to still offer God his dues of worship. I love that He made a decision to worship God even before knowing the outcome of the task. He tells his servants, "*...I and the young man will go yonder and worship...*" Abraham's attitude presents an emphatic resolve to fulfill his obligations as a son of God.

We can all learn from Abraham's commitment to the discipline of worship. Like Abraham, we have all felt the pressure of being weighted down from the worries of life. Times when it seems, before one storm passes another set of life events crash our efforts to rebuild a sense of stability. When moments like these arrive, it is imperative that we meet the storms with our mouths filled with worship. Worship keeps us balanced. Like medicine, it regulates the abnormalities in our lives then alleviates the ailments of living in this broken earthly vessel. God uses the act of worship to infiltrate our beings and re-establish His order within our lives. God wants to know that no matter what circumstances come our way we understand worship is not an option. It is a requirement to access upward levels in our lives. Upon the conclusion of Abraham's obedience, God spares Isaac's life. I believe God's request for Abraham to sacrifice Isaac was so He could test Abraham's loyalty to Him.

Worship is an act of obedience that we must not misinterpret as only an expressive emotional outcry. Worship can be carried out in many ways: listening to music, praying, or singing are common methods. However, we must not stop at those surface, yet impactful forms of worship. There are other unique ways to worship God. When we love our neighbors and give our lives to the service of others we are worshipping God. We worship Him through our lifestyle choices and obeying His will. Even further, paying our tithes and giving offering, honoring our bodies, and abstaining from unlawful sexual pleasures are examples of more practical ways to apply the act of worship into our lives.

God created each one of us as spiritual beings, able to connect to Heaven through our worship to Him. If you want to defeat Satan and advance to greater heights of your life engage in the art, act, and expression of obedience through a lifestyle filled with worship.

DEB'S DOWNLOAD

The wise will worship.

MIRROR CHALLENGE

Listen to "Holy Spirit You are Welcome Here" by Kim Walker

From the passages above, choose one way to worship God right now. Speak it aloud.

GET UP AND GO

"Give not [unnecessary] sleep to your eyes, nor slumber to your eyelids...Go to the ant, you sluggard; consider her ways and be wise! Which having no ruler or chief, overseer, or ruler, provides her food in the summer and gathers her supplies in the harvest. How long will you sleep, O sluggard? When will you arise out of your sleep? Yet a little sleep, a little slumber, a little folding of the hands to lie down and sleep — so will your poverty come like a robber or one who travels [with slowly but surely approaching steps] and your want like an armed man [making you helpless.]"

–Proverbs 6:4,6-11; Proverbs 24:33-34

"He becomes poor who works with a slack and idle hand, but the hand of the diligent makes rich."

–Proverbs 10:4

"The appetite of the sluggard craves and gets nothing, but the appetite of the diligent is abundantly supplied."

–Proverbs 13:4

"The sluggard does not plow when winter sets in; therefore he begs in harvest and has nothing."

–Proverbs 20:4

A friend once said to me, "So, Deborah, when are you going to write your first book?" I replied, "Um, I've been getting around to it. You know, jotting down ideas here and there." Then he said, "Well, you're a wonderful writer you should definitely complete it." To which I responded, "I will, one day. One day." This is a scenario in which I am all too familiar. The scene where my problem with procrastination is exposed and I try to explain it away. For as long as I can remember, I have waited until the last minute or until it was too late to complete tasks. Most commonly in the area of writing. In high school I took advanced english courses that required summer reading projects. It never failed, I would wait until the week before school started to crack open the book and finish the assignment. I am not kidding, every single paper—sadly including this book—have been written hours before the deadline. Though, I would always get an "A", this bad habit made me feel like it was an acceptable behavior.

When the Holy Spirit put it on my heart to write about procrastination I almost felt like a hypocrite. I wondered why He felt I was qualified to speak on such a topic, I mean He knows me very well, and this is one area I am certainly guilty. As I did my research in preparation to write, I realized that God knew in order for me to write on procrastinating, I would first have to consume the lesson for myself. Little did I know, the Bible *strongly* speaks on the topic of approaching life in this irresponsible manner.

King Solomon, definitely did not spare our feelings in warning us of the destitute future ahead if we do not acquire a good work ethic. "Sluggishness and poverty" are what he says we can look forward to with a life filled with procrastination. Ouch! The good news is, if you are like me, we are not cemented to the error of our ways. Thankfully, we have a friend in the ant. When showcasing the ants, the Bible highlights its tenacity. We see that an ant eats in the winter because it works in the summer to store up the food. It does not wait until the food is getting low to put its life matters in order; on the contrary, the ant is proactive in preparing. A major key in this verse is the line "which has no chief, overseer, or ruler", this implies that ants are built with the self-drive it takes to provide for itself. Now, if God instilled this measure of resourcefulness into an ant, how much greater has He placed inside of each one of us?

For me, this topic has yielded a high level of conviction. I believe a large part of our lives being unfulfilled is directly related to procrastination. Scripture is clear, "The appetite of the sluggard craves and gets nothing, but the appetite of the diligent is abundantly supplied." If we are suffering any lack, could it be that our appetites are craving what we are not willing to work for? Besides having a dream, how much effort have we put forth toward ensuring the dream comes to life? Are we waking up early to put time into it? Have we reorganized our lives so that the dream can be practiced and implemented? Today I challenge you, as I do myself, to consider the ant.

DEB'S DOWNLOAD

Work. Eat. Sleep.
Repeat

MIRROR CHALLENGE

Admit to yourself and write the areas in which you have been procrastinating.

For each area name a distraction that prevents you from completing the task.

Now, implement a strategy to avoid the distraction(s).

Share your strategies with your accountability partner from Day 16.

COME AND TAKE

"Come to Me, all you who labor and are heavy- laden and overburdened, and I will cause you to rest. [I will ease and relieve and refresh your souls.] Take My yoke upon you and learn of Me, for I am gentle (meek) and humble (lowly) in heart, and you will find rest (relief and ease and refreshment and recreation and blessed quiet) for your souls. For my yoke is wholesome (useful, good - not harsh, hard, sharp, or pressing, but comfortable, gracious, and pleasant), and My burden is light and easy to be borne."

–Matthew 11:28-30

Dealing with heaviness is an exhausting experience if we are not taught how to properly dispose of it. Thankfully, the Bible gives two specific instructions for dealing with the difficulties of burnout, "come" and "take". It is important to note, in this passage Jesus did not ask, He gave a decisive command. For people like me, who are givers and not so good receivers, this concept can be foreign. It's like, "So, God, you really want me to come to you, give you my bad stuff, then take your good stuff?" Yea, the logic just does not seem to add up, does it?

A little while ago, I found myself dealing with a lot of baggage and trying to handle it alone. I felt like I needed to be perfect and get all of my issues together before going to God. This could not have been further from the truth. After many sleepless nights, numerous migraines, and a lot of isolation, I finally decided to give God a try with my personal life. From the moment I genuinely told Him how I felt about everything I'd been dealing with and the parts I had played in the developments, the heaviness began to lift. To my surprise, God did not yell down from Heaven and send lighting to strike me to a far unknown place; rather, an insurmountable peace consumed me like never before.

I am learning that God does not want us to hide from Him and He most certainly does not want us walking around being ashamed of where we are in life. God wants us to know it is ok to show the authenticity of who we are, so that we will not be burdened with the weights of this world. Jesus took on our cares and sins with no cause other than love. Inasmuch as the Cross is inclusive of all who believe, it is just as exclusive to the individual. He died for me and you, personally. If I were the only person to come into this world, He would have still carried out Calvary because He loves me. Guess what, the same truth goes for you.

The Word tells us to "come to Him all you who are heavy-laden and burdened and I will give you rest." Because of Love, God likes for us to come raggedy and broken; then He exchanges our rags (lies, debts, mistakes, failures) for His riches (Love, Joy, Peace, Confidence). We must not allow shame and disappointment to get in the way of us going to the loving God's arms. When we make the exchange we then allow Him to put the pieces of our lives back together the way He sees fit.

DEB'S DOWNLOAD

Living in the world is simple when we carry out our job of coming to Him and taking on His presence.

MIRROR CHALLENGE

Admit to God how you really feel about the challenges in your life right now.

Next, listen to your favorite worship song.

Write down anything you hear during this time. Speak only the positive aloud.

GOD WILL HELP YOU

"If any of you is deficient in wisdom, let him ask of the giving God [Who gives] to everyone liberally and ungrudgingly, without reproaching or faultfinding, and it will be given him. Only it must be in faith that he asks with no wavering (no hesitating, no doubting). For the one who wavers (hesitates, doubts) is like the billowing surge out at sea that is blown hither and thither and tossed by the wind."
–James 1:5-6 (AMP)

The one commonality amongst every human being is pain. Satan uses the pain of our pasts, to infect our present, in order to destroy our future. Wow, I just said a mouthful, right? Let me say it again, Satan uses the pain of our pasts, to infect our present, in order to destroy our future. If we never settle or make peace with the decisions and the events that took place to help shape who we are today, then we will never be able to fully move forward into the bright future we desire.

Our pasts can either be ammunition for us to be stronger for today or it can be the kryptonite that weakens and stifles us into delay. It is our job to be able to face the pain of our past then move forward. I am not saying that the pain should not hurt, what I am saying is it should not handicap us. If we focus on the negative too long it becomes hard to get out of the dark place and to the place of Light. Ultimately, it is how we interpret the pain of the past, in the present, that will foster the growth needed to obtain our future.

The good news is, we have a Supreme being that will help us if we are willing to give Him the control. I believe many of us struggle with the pains of our past because we do not realize that we have a God that is not only able, but willing, to help us break free from all the pain and lead us into the best future, the future He talks about in Jeremiah 29:11. All we have to do is ask and believe that He will give it to us.

DEB'S DOWNLOAD

To ask for help is one of the strongest things we, humans, can do.

MIRROR CHALLENGE

Identify two key areas in your life that you can ask God for help. Write them down in your journal then speak the request aloud to God.

MAJOR IN THE MINOR

"My heart was touched and I fervently sang to him my desire] Take for us the foxes, the little foxes that spoil the vineyards [of our love], for our vineyards in blossom."

–Song of Solomon 2:15

As a dancer, an important component to bettering the craft is stretching; however, stretching is arguably the most underused technique amongst dancers across the globe. This is because it takes extra time before class, after class, and even outside of the studio. Stretching is recommended to be implemented daily, preferably multiple times. Now, if we look at dancers such as Misty Copeland, the first Black principal dancer for the American Ballet Theatre, we would discover a repertoire that includes stretching emphatically. This is because Misty has mastered the art of majoring on the minor, which requires clear-cut discipline. When we focus on perfecting the small details of our dreams, we are setting ourselves up to produce tailored results fitting for champions. If left unkempt, we run the risk of being restrained by our lackluster behaviors.

Like Misty, we have to ensure the most minute facets are being constructively molded into the best of our work. In other words, it is important to identify and focus on every detail of our business and dreams. In Song of Solomon 2, we see an exchange between two lovers. In verse fifteen, the female lover tells the male to "take for us the foxes, the little foxes that spoil the vineyards". The symbolism here is that though foxes are carnivorous animals, they still eat plants and grapes. Foxes are also known for being sly creatures, therefore their presence in a vineyard could be destructive. Basically the bride is saying to her husband, "Let's be sure that we focus on the small things that can destroy our relationship unexpectedly". Each one of us should adapt this same concept for our lives, not just in relationships but in all aspects, so that we, too, can obtain the greatest height of our abilities.

So Deborah, what do the small steps look like? That's a good question. For myself, in the quest to become a traveling speaker and touring author, I first have to ensure my content is as excellently polished as possible. I cannot wait until someone invites me to speak to develop speaking material. The product has to already be established, complete, and ready to present. Further, I have to ensure that I have marketed myself appropriately, which includes headshots. (Like who wants to take headshots?) However, these are professional images that represent who I am and my brand. Before I can seek representation, I must package a highlight demo of my working capabilities. This requires time for me to study monologue material to showcase my speaking abilities and professionalism. The preparation list goes on and on.

Many times we, especially millennials, prefer to cut corners to get to the top. We expect to have a dream, then wake up and live it, not understanding that if we arrive anywhere fast we will leave just as swiftly. As stretching is overlooked in dance because of time, we often try to skip over the small, important details because it requires our focus and uninterrupted effort. I pray we begin to understand in making the sacrifice, we become the masters of our crafts and better stewards of our abilities. Thereby placing ourselves in a secure position of earned ownership. I believe God wants us to perfect that which He has given to us in the proper way, one that will ultimately bring Him glory.

DEB'S DOWNLOAD

Ignored small steps lead to missed big steps. Stretch.

MIRROR CHALLENGE

Refer to the list you made in Day 20

Write down the small steps that can be implemented to accomplish your purpose? Speak them aloud, then get to work.

FAITH-FORWARD PROGRESSION

"Simon Peter replied, You are the Christ, the Son of the living God. Then Jesus answered him, Blessed (happy, fortunate, and to be envied) are you, Simon Bar-Jonah. For flesh and blood [men] have not revealed this to you, but My Father Who is in heaven. And I tell you, you are Peter [Greek, Petros— a large piece of rock], and on this rock [Greek, petra — a huge rock like Gibraltar] I will build My church, and the gates of Hades (the powers of the infernal region) shall not overpower it [or be strong to its detriment or hold out against it]."

–Matthew 16:16-18

Faith, one of those topics that gets generically covered in conversations about life, spirituality, and achieving dreams. Pastors scream it from pulpits; congregations shout about in the pews; business owners speak about it at seminars; teachers promote it in classrooms, and parents urge their children to keep hold of it on the path to adulthood. I thought faith was simply speaking what I wanted and expecting to see it based off of my words. I believed that as long as I spoke something it would be. However, as I have grown, I have become acquainted with the diverse complexities of Faith. I now know, it is not magical fairy dust we sprinkle over problems and situations in our life to make our dreams come true. It is not a wish we submit to a blue genie, nor is it a think-tank housing the good thoughts we seek to give mankind. I have learned that Faith requires effort, and it must be developed.

In football, there is a concept called forward progression. This occurs wherever the ball carrier catches the ball on the field and lands with both of his feet prior to being tackled by the defense.

This point is where the ball is considered dead until the next play, which will begin at this mark. This mark is declared based on the ball carrier's forward momentum and even if a defender hits the ball carrier and moves him backwards in yardage, it does not affect the forward progression. In many ways forward progression is the way our faith is designed to look.

The disciple Peter's life is a perfect example of forward progression because we get to see the four stages of the process acted out in Peter's faith dynamic. In Matthew 16:16-18, Peter catches the ball of belief. Though many were around, it was Peter who caught the understanding of who Jesus was, not by men's standard, but by God's. The second phase of Peter's forward progression occurs in Luke 22:31-32 when Jesus warns Peter about Satan's desire to destroy believers. Jesus goes on to tell Peter He's been praying for Peter's faith, that it would "not fail". The third step is when it is time to combat the defense. We see later in Luke 22 (v.54-62) that Peter did not stand his ground. His faith failed him and he denied Jesus. The scriptures say in v.62 that Peter "wept bitterly". Where was Peter's faith we saw in Matthew 16? It seems the defense had moved him in a backwards motion. There will be times in our walks of faith that we fall short and when, against our desires to do and be better, we choose to trade our Faith for an easier route. It is in these times, I believe, where the true depth of our character is revealed. Peter could have ran to hide, commit to a life of self-pity, or even did like Judas and killed himself. But he did not and as a result we remember Peter for more than his low moment of faith.

Just as on a football field, no matter how far the defense pushes you backwards, what counts is where you first catch the ball and land. Peter caught the ball when He confessed to Jesus who He was, so even in the moment where he denied Him not once, not twice, but three times, what mattered was that his moment of forward progression had already been established. Therefore, after Jesus' death and resurrection, Peter was able to implement step four of forward progress, he took his rightful place. He was the first disciple to operate in the power of what he learned from walking with Jesus. In Acts chapter 2, we see that Peter delivers the first sermon documented in the New Testament by anyone other than Jesus. Peter acknowledges who Jesus was and what

He did, not only that, 3000 people came to Christ. This was all because Peter decided to implement his forward progression. He did not let his huge mistakes discount him from taking his rightful place. In doing so he was able to fulfill Jesus' words "and I tell you, you are Peter, and on this rock I will build My church". We see here that forward progression led Peter to become one of the most influential figures in the New Testament.

Like Peter, we must not ever let life, Satan, or even ourselves, prevent us from fulfilling our greatest potential. We cannot allow what seems to be slow progress deny our ability to advance forward. While operating in the action of Faith, our life's journey will unquestioningly bring obstacles and forceful opposition that can cause us to experience setbacks and delays. Similar to the defensive and offensive play of a football team. However, we must be courageous enough to believe that we are more than the lowest moment. When the whistle has blown and the defense has paused, we must advance to the location of our forward progression.

DEB'S DOWNLOAD

Progress forward

MIRROR CHALLENGE

Listen to "Moving Forward" by Israel Houghton

Consider the 4 stages of Forward Progression:

1. *The Catch*
2. *The Warning*
3. *The Battle*
4. *The Advance*

Based on the list above, which stage are you in life? Write it down.

If you are in the third stage, list ways you can progress forward?

RISE

"And when Jesus came to the ruler's house and saw the flute players and the crowd making an uproar and din, He said, Go away; for the girl is not dead but sleeping. And they laughed and jeered at Him. But when the crowd had been ordered to go outside, He went in and took her by the hand, and the girl arose. And the news about this speed through all that district."

–Matthew 9:23-26

One day, while living in Houston and walking near the lake in the neighborhood, I saw a huge turtle near the playground at the clubhouse. Initially, I thought it was one of those tricky garden decorations, that is, until the turtle's neck snapped back into its shell and scared the living daylights out of me. After realizing that it was alive and taking a moment to be amazed by its beauty, I realized that the turtle was in this awkward position because its legs were stuck in the mud so it could not free itself. Deciding not to leave the helpless creature to fend for itself, or falsely assume someone else would come by to help him, I picked up a stick to lift the turtle out of its elements. As I preceded to lift the turtle by the back of the shell something interesting happened. Each time I used an upward motion, the turtle would use an opposing motion to hunker down causing it to sink further into the mud. By this time the turtle's neck had retreated almost fully back into its shell, making it more difficult to assist him. Finally, I was able to use the stick to levy him out of the hole he'd dug while trying to get himself out. After gaining his composure, the turtle trekked slowly off into the woods.

As I began to think about the turtle I considered how reflective the experience is of human behavior. Sometimes life has a way of making us feel stuck in bleak situations. In Matthew 9:23-26, we see a similar situation. A young girl has died and there is a crowd of mourners around. These mourners cannot help the situation, they are only there to fulfill the customary duties during death in that time. In the text, we see Jesus tell the crowd to "go away; for the girl is not dead but sleeping". Although it may seem crazy, I believe that we have to approach our dead situations with the same certainty Jesus approaches this girls' body. He knew the plans and intentions God created for this young girl were not finished; therefore, she could not be dead, only resting. Later in the passage, after the crowd is ordered out, Jesus goes in takes her by the hand and the girl arises. I love that the account does not mention a struggle for the girl to come back to life, rather that it was a simple three step process. Jesus went in, took her by the hand, and she rose. I believe many of us would have responded to Jesus the way the turtle responded to me. We would have found reasons to shrink back and stay in our space of despair, making it more difficult for the help sent to get us out of our bad situations.

A little while ago I had an awakening moment like the little girl had with Jesus. When faced with so many obstacles and situations that felt immovable, I found myself not wanting to live. I did not want to continue in the efforts of building my life and living in eternity seemed to be the only way for me to imagine a life worth living. Like the little girl, it was not until the crowds in my life began to leave did I experience Jesus walking into my deathly situation, grabbing me by the hand, and raising me up. No, Jesus did not literally come from the sky and appear to me. However, He did bring the right people in my life at just the right time. For example, through a sequence of unexplainable events, in the midst of a crowd of 20,000 people, I met the head of a counseling department for a large counseling center in Houston. She and I began to walk through the dark thoughts I was experiencing. I began to see the effects of Jesus raising me up. I learned that if we allow someone to help us, despite the fear we feel, we can go further than we could have gone on our own.

There are many excuses we use to retreat when help comes our way. I believe this is because we unconsciously become comfortable in the shell of poverty, brokenness, self-sabotage, defeat, and negative thinking. We hold on to these false ideals as truth then establish our lives in the depths of those realities. I believe it is important for us to remember that Jesus can and will send help masked in people, opportunities, jobs, and experiences. We must not be closed to doors of God's divine miracles. It is even more important to remember that we can arise because Jesus has "chosen, appointed, and planted us to bear lasting fruit that will honor and glorify" God. Our lives are to so mirror the image of Jesus that, just as He rose from the grips of death, we too should rise from every deadly thing we face to live life victoriously. When we find ourselves in situations like the turtle we must respond like the girl in Matthew and rise.

DEB'S DOWNLOAD

Resist the urge to go into your shell. Rise!

MIRROR CHALLENGE

Listen to "Rise" by Andra Day

1. *In what areas have you become like the turtle?*
2. *How has Jesus sent help your way? Have you utilized the help?*

Speak ways you can use your help aloud.

Conclusion

Congratulations, you have concluded The 30-Day Speak Life Challenge!

Thank you for entrusting the last 30 days of your life to me and the Use Your Words journey. Not for a moment do I take this for granted. When writing this book, my intentions were not to create another self-help-super-spooky-super-spiritual-unachievable-idealistic resource that flies over the heads of the masses. Instead, I sought to create a work that aided in your ability to implement measurable steps to better your approach to life.

I pray I have done so. I pray that you are committed now, more than ever, to think more kindly about your purpose on earth. I pray that you are speaking life in every arena pertaining to your existence. I pray more that you are committed to sustaining this way of living. This, my friend, is only the beginning. The road ahead is sure to be filled with many loopholes and surprises, however, with the right thinking and speaking it is bound to be a wonderful adventure. I urge you to continue practicing your new ways, if not, your old ones will creep back in. If this happens though, and you find yourself in a slump, do not panic, just repeat the process...for 30 days.

Finally, it has been my pleasure to serve through my life in preparation for this work. I did not know that every deplorable and happy experience was grooming me to better serve you. Now, that I know, it has all been worth it; every tear, every frustration, every broken relationship, every moment of weakness and insecurity. It was all worth "growing" through because I have become better to help someone like me. Imagine if we all lived this way, a world where each one lived as though their existence mattered to another. What humble servants and gracious leaders we would have fostered. I cannot thank you enough for forcing me to become everything Earth requires of me. Never forget, we speak life to serve.

Yours in His Service,

About the Author

Deborah is...

a living-breathing example of the wind. She spends most days with her computer, a cup of tea, and FaceTiming friends and family. She is a minister of dance, praise and worship leader, motivational speaker, and social entrepreneur.

Deborah is a graduate of the University of Southern Mississippi with a Bachelor's of Science in Business Administration with an emphasis in Tourism. In 2014, Deborah started Deborah Quave Enterprises, LLC, the parent company for her business ventures. As founder and CEO she launched "Use Your Words The Movement". Through Use Your Words she works as a mentor, blogger, editor, and broadcasting personality. Since the inception of Use Your Words, she has delivered her messages of communicative restoration in schools, youth programs, retreats, and conferences. She combines her background in technology with her program development and event planning skills to present self-enhancement initiatives through the company.

Deborah hosts Use Your Words nationwide prayer calls where hundreds of young adults have come together to pray. She led the Covenant of Love Church worship team in Houston, Texas and Friday Night Harvest Watch with I Love New York. She has danced with christian dance companies in Ocean Springs, MS, Atlanta, GA, Birmingham, AL, Hammond, LA., Los Angeles, CA., and Puerto Rico. Most notably, she was a featured dancer on the Sea of Galilee in Israel. She delivered her inaugural sermon at The Rock Church in South Pasadena, CA.

Deborah lives with a mission to die empty and to spread love to every person she meets.

Contact

To contact Deborah for speaking or dance ministry engagements, questions, and/or prayer requests log onto www.useyourwords-themovement.com or email info@useyourwordsthemovement.com.

Facebook
www.facebook.com/Deborah.Quave

Instagram
@DeborahQuave

Twitter
@DeborahQuave

Made in the USA
Columbia, SC
20 September 2020